POEMS

ALL THINGS BRIGHT

&

QUADRILLE FOR TIGERS

T0164040

CHRISTINE CRAIG: POEMS

ALL THINGS BRIGHT

&

QUADRILLE FOR TIGERS

PEEPAL TREE

First published in Great Britain in 2010
Peepal Tree Press Ltd
17 King's Avenue
Leeds LS6 1QS
UK

Quadrille for Tigers
was first published in 1984
by Mina Press
Berkeley, California

ISBN 13: 9781845231729

Supported by
ARTS COUNCIL
ENGLAND

For my dearly beloveds:

Rachael and Rebecca

Maxine and Penny

Joshua and Sarah

ALL THINGS BRIGHT

QUADRILLE FOR TIGERS

ALL THINGS BRIGHT

PART 1.

SWEET FRUIT

SWEET FRUIT

She was stern, you know,
upright, a woman alone, a trifle
proud. He came to the door, one foot
then both, rocking gently in
an old chair, his voice low, swift
like birds, like rivers.

She kept a safe distance though
slowly old ties were loosening
fluttering round her heart; years
reserves, cautions melted,
slid through veins, sifted through pores
gone, in a faint smell of leaves and mist.

He came closer, twined stories
in the curls about her neck
hung poems, the first diamonds of
her life, around her ears and pressed
his name upon her hesitant mouth.
Say it all, tell it clear, he said.

The past whirls, scarred, pitted,
pockmarked like a planet
far away in a dark night.
Oppressed by too many years
of silence, quiet as a leaf
as family raged in a shabby home
that groaned under the weight
of too much ego, too much rum.

Pull away, quiet as a leaf
in the school that sheltered
growing girls from the sun of

an island, covering a violent past
in noisy new growth. Hush,
for the teachers are teaching
and success comes to those
who can learn Latin and Chaucer,
take x to the power of y.

In escape are many degrees of
silence; the best settles softly
in the old chapel where the child
sings, soaring with psalms, or
in the one-room library dreams
as the quiet of a country afternoon
slips past trees through valleys
starred with flame where flowers
open their silky throats to die.

The child is a woman who
has not learned to speak
so her freedom drifts to others.
No, shame halts the pen
halts the telling.

Take then a different kind
of stillness, a silence in which
words bloom, burst out
raking over old angers
burning up feelings so long
shut out they became monsters,
child's nightmares in an adult bed.
Turn them out with the nice girl
who silenced them. Say them,
speak them, cry them.

Out of the void the planet moves
nearer, scarred, but trembling

with energy.
New words come,
words to build
a new heart
a new home.

These lovers, mulatto children
oceans apart, but crossing and
re-crossing the imagination,
the past weaves time up between them
alive, gleaming, a shared shawl to hold
them warm for the present.
The future, the grandparents
had so little regard for it.

Ancestral roamings, who knows of
the homelands in Africa, distant,
for in the families they speak of
the lighter side of things, preferring
frankly not to delve too far on either
side as the Irish family may contain
its crop of drunkards and the Portuguese
may be a vagabond sailor turned linen-
suited merchant in the tropics.

Ancestral roamings, forced, favoured,
leave a trail of restlessness. Fanning
out all classes travel – bags, grips,
boxes ready in every household. Kamau
you made the beat of it reverb in us.
London, New York, setting down to set up
rice and peas, roti, reggae an
rass man nostalgia. Stay, stay
she wants to say, but tracks cut in
the shared memory, are clearer than
home-trod paths to Georgetown, Kingston,

Bridgetown, the very names resolutely
town, not big city, big money foreign.

Stay, for here we have been young
splashing at the standpipe
jostling for places at school
and so vulnerable; and who
in the streets of London
in the subways of New York
knows your tree-climbing
sling-shot, kite-flying,
rope-skipping days as we do.

And is it just gaff, old talk
or is it the very shape of your face
the curve of your arm
the way your eyes look out
at the world that was made
in those days. And for the
many who were hungry, for
the many who were abused
who grew like weeds with
prickle-bush in the heart
for the beatings and the
absence of a soft voice
stay, for here is home,
here is yourself facing
yourself every day, having
to love yourself or you
will wither in the cold
your heart will shrink
to an old rag
fluttering
on the grey train lines
to nowhere.

For here is somewhere
with the Red Stripe bang
on the table loud
as the domino you know
will win. Here is music for
stepping and rocking
and bluesing down
a sweet girl, and here is
yourself sweating on the bus
leaning into every curve
and here is politics talk
that matters, for it's your
child can't find place in school
your mother can't find bed
in hospital, and your endless love
and frustration that you can speak:
Bwoy, it dread iyah.
True word.

He puts his mouth close to her heart,
his lips an arrow of heat in her blood.
Fly, he says. See your wings wrenched
from red dirt, dried in the morning sun.
I saw when you rolled them in the sea
to set their sparkling colours. I felt when
you shook them in the roaring waterfall
and hung them on the mountains to dry.

WESTMORELAND

In Westmoreland, an old great house,
the housekeeper wears a jangle of keys.
Intercede with her, please, for a spoon,
for a plate, each locked away in separate
compartments. At night I hear
the slaves weeping in the canes,
a steady, fearful weeping all night long.
It is horror. The weight of the past
in that house and me, product of both,
red chile in the master's bed, sweating
with the loathing of it. Homeless, no
dark London street, no grimy subway
holds that sharp no place, no fit,
no home, weeping in the blood.

Black housekeeper says, half timid,
half defiant, she has a coolie man.
Not good status round here, but
he's kind to her, she says.
Oh lady, love that coolie man,
history towers behind him,
spiritual flowers yearned
for by restless intellects
are his, by birth, by race,
by years lit by a love of God
so profound it made deathless songs
for mind, heart and soul to know
one shining harmony.

"God made the rivers to flow
they find no weariness, they
cease not from flowing. They
fly swiftly like birds in the air.

May the stream of my life flow
into the rivers of righteousness..."

Light a candle here for the souls
of the slaves, for Krishna striding
through the canes to bless us. Africa
and India yoked here in
children and rum shops and
lovers' beds, in small houses and
large fields and the beauty of
having come through, come through
hard times and plantation
to this rich yielding land where black
is a song of understanding
and red is a part of the version,
part of the lyrics of discovery.

KINGSTON

In a chic apartment high above the waterfront
an irritable intellectual looks over
the streets of Kingston, labels them definitively
Dante's *Inferno*. His book-lined walls stand
an army of soldiers to protect his troubled
sleep, yet he plans another flight. He can't
stay, too provincial, violent, threatening.
He can't quite leave either.

Estelle irons khaki and navy
blue for school tomorrow.
Need a school shoes for Rosie.
A which part Sam gone? Dem
so sweet when dem a hunt you
down and swift as chicken hawk
fe gone when dem get you.
Seem like gone is a word spell wid
a *m* and a *a* and a *n*.

Estelle fights her way in
the minibus uptown to look
a work. No work. Me can sew
you know, Mam. No work. Me can
bake an cook and clean floor
till you see you face inna it.
No work. Estelle with housekeeping
skills and no house to keep
only empty cupboards, cold stove
and children soon reach home
hungry. Swallow you pride girl
go see you sister Norma.
You know say she a go harass
out you soul case but blood
thicker dan water.

Mornin Norma, how you keepin?

Norma is keeping an office job
and church on Sunday, looking
for a fine upright man. Norma
is studying books at night-school
and every day planning how
to move up, how to talk good
so nobody will know seh
is Jones Town she coming from.
What happen, Estelle, you see
me name bank? When you a lie down
wid different man you don't tink
bout how you a go manage.

Estelle, star of heartbreak
prefers learning the no job
pavements step by step, edging
past the mad sculptor who creates
with boxes and signs, with old shoes
and rags carefully shaped round
a leafless tree. Walking home
with dollar cornmeal and Marley
catching at the edges of her mind:
who feel it knows it Lord.

Weep, weep for us women on the streets
of Kingston. Weep for our children
hungry, angry in this town that blooms
large houses, smooth lawns where other
children play computer games and plan
the next trip to Miami.
Weep, but also watch Estelle, dark star
in an anguished sky. No poem,
no politics, no church, no way to close
this wound, only an endless searching

seeking to meet ourselves
greet ourselves, honourably.

ST. THOMAS

It starts out well, lush
tangled, then flat into cane
sugar, crop of foreign sweetness.
Here it is bending and saw-edge
of leaf cutting years into body
sun a machete of heat in the head.
Further up is Bogle country
but here charters signed
bruckins in Spanish Town Square
are far away, never happened;
cane arrows brush history back
to books, pale heads arrogant
in an empty sky.

Drums, drums and hips thrusting
in Kumina, roll back the sea
to Africa, only coming back each day
fears, love, vengeance tread deep paths
to obeah man's red flag house.
At night, home is a row
of black hovels, the sight of it
the shame of it stabbing shards
in the staring eye, year after year
as babies grow old and die.

Inland, fields of dairy cattle, promise
of better jobs, and patches of rich farmland,
sturdy homes mocking the faded gentility
of Bath mineral spa, ancient palms
watchful over Bligh's mutinied buds.
All that coolness lost on the rock
beat of coast, flat salt ponds
lick white, parched lips sorrowing
for the dry absence of birds.

Yet stop here for golden honey
little brown breasts of naseberries
sweet, grainy on the tongue. Flushed
cheeks of mangoes and black-eyed
sweetsops piled high on a makeshift
roadside table. Sweet fruit, hard life.

ST. ANN SATURDAY

Saturday afternoon, so many shades
of black swinging down the road.
Funeral time.
Nice afternoon she get, eh!

If.

An so many smady turn out
like a old days' funeral.

Dats right.

Imagine her time come
so quick. Well, de Lord giveth
an de Lord taketh away.

Amen Sister.

Children walk lightly, plaits
floating with rainbows of ribbons
beside auntie's strong hips; uncle's
suit so dark his body is held in tight,
moves only back, front, front, back.
Auntie's hips roll sedately, heave
like waves beside the dancing plaits.

You see her big daughter come from
Canada. Me no like how she look
at all. No sir. She look a way.
Me never member sey she so mawga.
Me mind tell me she catching
hard times over dere.

Mebbe so an mebbe not.

Six pickney Miss Martha
raise, she one bring dem up
an send dem into de world.
Six pickney, she one,
an is one degge, degge daughter
come home fe bury her.
Still an all, dem neva come
when she was hearty,
no mek sense dem come
when she direckly dead.

A dat too.

Starapple leaves, double toned,
bend quiet over the steady walking
walking for Miss Martha, gone to rest.
The path she walked, food to market,
children to school, Sunday to church,
steady walking. In the end, alone
under the starapple leaves, a hush
fell over her, silence of age,
of no names left to call
to table. Of no news from
Delroy or Maisie or Petal
or Lennie or Edith or Steve.

Nice turnout Miss Martha have.
Nuh Granny Bailey dat from Retreat?
Well I neva. Tink sey she dead
long time. Time passing chile,
we all moving down de line weself.

True word.

DISCOVERY BAY

On this beach the figure sets feet
calmly into powdered coral, silicates,
horned shells and fragments of wood.
Here, on this shore, under webbed
sea grape leaves, time feels, smells
as it did years ago. Sand has the same
lustre and sudden dull crescents when
blue tongues, lightly foamed with white
lick quickly inland.

The same when boots
and sea-dirty horse
strode to a meeting,
the agenda
plunder.

Brown feet stood soft here
and gave way, gave way
to white and black,
their whispering
and clashing
rippled over the sighing cane,
mingled with
the arrivings
and escapes
of those who moved
through the arches of this sea.

Cathedrals, stained glass and years
nestle mustily in sculpted
corners, like algae on rocks.
Wooden pews remain straight-
backed defying the sour notes
of history sounding just past

the door. Laid to rest now
under wingless angels and urns
garlanded with stone roses.
Oh God our help in ages brushes
past the scrolled tablets and is lost in
the rolling of the sea. All history,
all secrets laid to rest, here
where children's toes curl brown
in a past powdered into sand,
scooped into shells that curve
by the child's ear. She listens,
her eyes glimmer
and grow old quickly.

PORTLAND MORNING

Sea swallowed up the night
trees sprung out, pole-vaulted
into blue, an endless domed blueness
of morning. Dwarfed, workers pick
their way down stony paths to wait,
brightly clumped, for country buses.

The morning starts slowly for them
but in the fields sweat rolls down
muscled backs or spreads through
shapeless, no-colour work shirts.
Two women and a child pile sand,
cart it away in head-loads, so thin
dark arabesques of life sentenced
on this endless beach to hard labour.

But round a corner spotless white villas
guard entry to the lagoon. Stretching
from soft beds, guests take coffee
on the terrace, flutter a greeting with
smooth hands, red-tipped at the nails.
Oh world, a heart could break here,
only the lagoon, inventing endlessly
the colour blue, stills all thought,
empties the mind with one stroke.

How tall the trees stretch
wearing borrowed vines
throwing a languid arch
of branch towards
the leaf-steeped path.
Do you remember
in a hidden curve
how the springs pulsed

up, how the light spread
in flickering squares
mullioned windows of water
the blue there
a hardly blue, a just
barely there blue
washed out from
the palette of the sky?

The glory and thunder of
Boston Beach all
tumbling and ardent
waves and sun-heat
on white beach, and
echoing spray of
rolling sea, and
children black against
the open light and boys
riding, turn of the hips
curving in the surfboard
princes of this kingdom
of moving blueness, and
lovers turning golden
brush salty lips
lace fingers lightly
in the yielding sand.

The chair is still; the voice swift
as birds, as rivers, is gone.
Islands are every shape, every
colour of goodbye.
Walk good. See you next year
if life spare. Staying is
a quiet house, lonely a cord
to tie the night in knots,

even out the days to a grey stone.
But staying is also looking here
at these hills, learning the songs
of this sea, that flower opening
in the evening air, these children
whose beauty turns leaves of light
in the heart, in the mind.

PART II

LITHOGRAPHS

LITHOGRAPHS

Twilight.
We walk through a severe garden
to a wattle and daub house.
A very old woman in spotless white
sits propped up in bed waiting
with a smile for death.
Her skin is polished mahogany,
lids so hooded the eyes are a gleam
without shape.
Her voice is a rustle of birds' feathers
as they settle in the sunset to roost.

Twilight.
Sitting in Auntie's bed recovering
from malaria. Shadows fall from
spread breadfruit leaves into a
closed courtyard where Eva moves
with soft briskness to share the
evening meal, and the child hopes
she can spend another day in the
shuttered upstairs room with the
hush of tops of trees and the smooth
comfort of sun-scented sheets.

Twilight.
And only a second ago the sun
flared across Kingston harbour
to drop far away into cane fields,
and night licks up the last wisps
of orange cloud with a smooth, grey tongue.

A HOUSE WITH A BRIDGE

A house with a bridge
flowers spread in the sun.
Children stretch shapely limbs
run with shining, dimpled smiles.
Fruit of the womb
fruit of the lives
that glide in the home
with a bridge.

Broken fences, and the yams
didn't come to much this year,
and the trees have a blight
that speckles the leaves and
fruit droop, dripping wormy
juices on withered grass.

Same house, same land
the woman walks, walks at night,
walks with her child where the
floorboards creak, walks where
spiders spin shadows on shadows.

Dawn, a quick energy bursts
in her brain. She runs, leaves
snap in her hands, arms full of
green, crushed fragrant for a bath.
There now, there now and the child
sweats and wails. There now,
and he squirms, but she holds,
holds him close as he shivers,
shivers with fever draining away.
There now and his skin cools
cheeks round again, glowing.

A house with a bridge
where the children climb,
lay their arms plump by the
swelling fruits. Tendrils curl
greenly from the yams, close
where beans split their pods
with quick, red smiles
and the woman hums
an old song without words.

DIARY OF A DISTURBANCE

On Martin Luther King's birthday,
reading an anthology:
Item: the Caribbean poet is in England
writing of damp, smooth landscapes.
Item: the English poet is in a hot land
writing of a delicate whore
with lemon-scented hair.

Here the smoke from a day of roadblocks
hangs lightly over the city.
Dollar down, prices rising like bread
we can't afford to buy.
Roadblock Tuesday. Marley
would have known how to
make a song of this grief,
this island smothered by
experts, economists who
reduce us to negative growth
while we burn our rage
in piles of debris.

The radio DJs keep things moving.
Children at the police station;
please collect them, Mrs. M.
Husband can't get home tonight;
don't worry, Mrs. N.
Five year old Denise is missing...
Two women pick their way past
smoking tyres; the radio blares.
Many rivers to cross
and I can't seem to find...

Between mounds of broken bottles
boys play football in streets
empty of traffic. At twilight
on Martin Luther King's birthday
a sudden quiet descends.
Crowds drift home to a frugal supper
peace fans out over the hot streets.

The Caribbean writer muses over
wet landscapes. The English writer
plays with foreign dreams.
Here in the anthology of our life
we watch rage and frustration
take to the streets, and say
children's prayers on
Martin Luther King's birthday.

IVORY BEADS

Creamy white curls of elephant tusks,
ivory beads from Ethiopia.
My father played the piano –
jazz, swing – it had a round, fat
rousing sound; the energy of it
stayed long after the notes fell silent.

As a prim adolescent I stumbled
over Bach, became overly delicate
with Mozart and, stroking the ivories
thought romance pure, abstract
flowing through time
remote from reality.

Cool spheres of white, the devout
roll their fingers caressing the
Hail Marys the Lord is with thee,
or hang them crucified on a nail
by the bed in one-room shacks
from Peru to Portugal, or rest them
gleaming by bible and lace mantilla
in the perfumed homes
of the blessed rich.

Ivory beads from Ethiopia
children's teeth rot in the drought
mother's tears glitter among the flies:
the continent of all resources sends
precious trinkets to the West.
Thank you for the gift of ivory beads;
my conscience is troubled, they
slip so cool around my neck.

AN EVEN SHAPE

Her garden looks in through my window
crisscrossed by the white lattice.
Coolers, they call them but they are also
hiding places for young girls playing.

Her garden stands neatly round her house,
travels politely onto the verandah
to sit in pots or hang leafily down
from large earth-coloured urns.

She lives with Mama, shepherding with her full body
the hesitant ins and outs of Mama's half-blind days,
feeding her frail consciousness with edited *Gleaner* news
and homemade chicken soup.

In her home, borrowed children touch her china birds
with hands wiped clean from eating sticky cakes
and little pies, each with a cherry on the top,
or press moist, breathless kisses round
the corners of her smile.

Sometimes she fills the spaces out
with music, nostalgia floating in on
strings and flutes, old-fashioned love songs
of blue moons and forever and until.

Shameful peeping Tom, I sit silent in my lattice
watching the even shape of her days,
waiting to catch, just once, a wider open door
behind her steady eyes.

OFRENDA*

I am making an ofrenda for you, my sister,
for us, the dark and the light,
for yellow birds on the grass
and feathers stuck in oranges and how
we threw them to the sun to catch more colour
as they spiralled back to us.

And my ofrenda is white dresses for church
and coffee roses with satin-white petals and oh!
the thick green leaves of them and the sound of cows
swishing out to pasture in the red-dirt morning.

I'm making an ofrenda for you, my sister,
for the thief who stole your smile and how
we grew silent stumbling into adulthood
and lost our way too many times.

And I'm making this for all the small girls
gone too quiet, for the ones too willing
to be a should of this or a must of that,
for the many taught to hold their vessels
wide open for some other to fill.

I'm making an ofrenda for you, my sister,
for the making that we have as ours
for our fingers' damp sienna
scraping out the silt now
where the otherness was
smoothing the edge cracked now
where the dreams drained out.

But slap it on now, earth of our life
the bowl of our being ours to fill
with songs or silence
with rocks or roses
with hot salty kisses or
bright honey of children's laughter.

And I'm making an ofrenda for you, my sister,
for we have drawn the same months
and years of breath yet too often wept alone,
and my ofrenda is this: a strong sun and red lands
roses and yellow birds, and all in it a laughing
pleasure that we have known this together.

*Spanish: a roadside shrine erected to honour a deeply loved relative.

BUTTERFLY SEASON AT ST. HUGH'S

First they were caterpillars
horribly agile, curling in
viscous arcs from blue-starred
lignum vitae. Teacher threatened,
Be quiet or you'll stand
under the tree. Tomorrow's
doctors, lawyers, managers
and mothers bent quickly
silent heads to books.

Suddenly they are yellow
fluttering clouds over
the girls in green, who drift
like leaves blown from class
to class or, swept by an invisible
gardener, rest in mounds, voices
rustling in the sun.
Only sometimes, this girl
or that falls silent, caught
in the magic of it,
the school year turning
in trembling, transient
waves of winged sunshine.

POEMS FOR TWO DAUGHTERS

I.

We let each other go
for the journey you took
those shining eyes of childhood
that lit all my growing.
This winter night
far from you, they are
my benediction, fire-
light in my soul.
My first born love,
thinking of you my heart
trembles. How wise you are
and beautiful.

for Rachael

II

My daughter lends me her boots
it will be cold she says.
I slip my feet in and feel
the square, sure foot,
leather worn soft
at the instep.
Once her foot fit in my palm.
Oh, my lovely grown girl,
how warmed I am by you.

for Rebecca

CAPTIVE AUDIENCE

Lord I hate volubility
especially in the "learned",
streams of talk, great users
of parentheses, repetitions
like a faded Mexican blanket
worn of its colour, symbols
no longer radiant with meaning.

The men with soft voices
are the worst. No space
in the velvety folds to
get a word in. Pardon, my house
is on fire... As I mentioned
earlier... Hard to be downright
rude – one's upbringing brings
one down to the role of
captive audience, face swamped
with a soggy smile.

Ah the tyranny of the great talker,
the sadistic pleasure of forcing
the listener into helpless bondage,
groping feverishly for exit lines.
Listeners of the world unite!
Cast off the shackles of lingual oppression!
Strike now and establish your right
not to be bored to death. To bolster
your resolve, whisper this incantation:
Give me, oh Lord, a kind man,
one who can listen and talk
in equable proportions, one who
is free from the sin of repetition,
and please, Lord, one with whom
I can enjoy the voluptuous pleasure
of silence.

LONGING

Longing for comfort like
clean sheets, friends laughing
table set with candles, lit.
Longing – the word pries open soft
underbelly of sea urchin that is
so many women. Plastic armour
of rollers bending over a tray of
two, three icy mints
and single stick cigarettes,

Lady in pearls and satin hair,
cool in high-style, bullet-grey Benz
yet slips in grey eel of longing
probing her Dior shaded eyes
where hunger hides in shuttered pupils
for the child too late to have,
for the man not yet met.

Ah, even the old widow, back crusted
with arthritis, creaks into a straight
chair sifting sadly through memories,
too many not quite glorious, too many
dimmed by time to sea weed, all of
a colour. She too longs to sit
with a friend, trusted to cherish
her, remember her, black hair,
proud brown shoulders waltzing
in silver lamé at the Myrtle Bank.

FILM SCRIPT

Desolate, this time of rainfall
streets rich with brown rivers
where cars churn and sputter
or pause watchfully on one bank
gauging the best route to make it
safe to the other side.

Desolate, these streets of begging
children with scaly skin and small
malnourished limbs, a plea stamped
on their aging faces. Don't want it
the weight of this grief,
the stress of this country.

Must go, must move, must break
this stasis, this gloom where
day ends too early
night falls too swift.
Must go where women
are plowing the fields
patting tender seedlings
into deep, earth smell.
Must go where birds call
from high mountain trees
and coffee blossoms curve
white stars in a fallen sky of lilies.

Must go where fishermen spread
their nets in a dark vigil
and later pour their dancing
catch into noise and baskets
and cries of the market.

Admit
these summoned, ordered images
a film of longing through which
the real landscape grows, glows
bright in this shadowed time.

BI-FOCALS

A room, wine golden in
our laughing throats
love is sunny afternoons and
eating fish caught fresh and
firm, small tomatoes (how the
colour touches your lips) and love is
silence, reading by a shared lamp
your feet too long for the bed
and love is scarlet petals on my breast
and love is
someone close by
wearing
a necklace of lies.

THIS SKY THIS DAY

The beautiful girls
their smiles constellations
in mamas' sky, laughing
a story remembered from
plump and anxious days;
now it is a new boy charmed
a first job, college, all shrieks
and teasing, all lights flashing
and the music of their voices.

The mamas sit, beautiful too
a shapely arm, a greying curl
laugh lines growing between us
so close we are pearly onion skins
folded into each other; mothers
and daughters, we can no longer love
only this one with my name,
that one with your name, but all
they are our shining heaven.

This sky this day
who is giver
who receiver
who has yesterday
who tomorrow?
The allness of us
flows on, flows on.

TRAVELLING

Going out on my own,
friends flutter fears, dark
mutters fill ears tuned now
for other sounds, sounds of yes
the end sibilant with promise.

My dear friend is going.
His step is now light,
now hesitant, but he goes
legs muscled with energy,
pushing the door to smiles
at ticket counter, smiles
at steps of silver bird.
The airport churns heartbeats
through shaded exits into
the bright light of flight.

Go. And God go with you.
Nothing lasts, I said,
and you believed me.

Going out on my own.
Through the leaves shadows
fall on my heart. A bird,
softly grey, plumes past.
My breath catches, snags
with the weight of loss.
Go. And God go with you.
Only wish for me sunlight
sparkling on my feet.
Going out on my own.

ISLANDS

In St. Kitts a child stops,
turns back to smile full
into my eyes, her face
a dark flower with sun
on her lashes. For that moment
my face in the shade, yours
in the sun, my years, your youth
recognition trembles between us.

You pause, just ready to grow up.
Your smile says – I will be a woman
like you; my smile says, you are
pure delight. In that flash
of love and homage we know
it is sweet to be female.

In the curve of the beach
in the swell of hills
in the flush of orchids
in the tangled rain forests
in the sweet order of farmlands,
see across these islands
our daughters are growing
all our beauty
all our riches
are one.

PART III

THE STRANGER

THE STRANGER

She came to an island lost in
dust and drought. A stranger
seeking meaning from images, looking
for comfort in the smiles of men.
They smile, they promise, they
sigh… while the real women
in their lives take their real
children to school, nourish
their husbands' egos, hopes
faithful to an image of success
they contracted to bolster
years before under white net
and pink rosebuds.

In a dark room the stranger
is the freedom not to have
to speak of love which smells
now like a child's battered
lunch box with juice stains
and crumpled ends of stale
sandwiches, escape from the
mortgaged, tender smiles of wives,
from familiar rooms where manhood
is proved in bed, in the bank,
in the circle of similar friends.

From the stranger they seek
passion not cloaked with
ownership. The stranger gives
and smiles and goes away.
In the streets, the men without
jobs, without homes, without cars
stake out their territory,
their only ownership

themselves —
themselves blown up cinema size
by charm, hostility, macho words
centred on a woman's blood.

What blighted our men that
they cannot love, that sex is
a hoe for planting seeds left
untended, to straggle up like
weeds till they too seek their
manhood in loveless couplings?
Or sex is seeking strangers
while the wife gives the baby
to the nursemaid and wonders
why the crisp new office job
opens another empty space
in her heart.

Guilt sweeps the stranger like a wave
surging, retreating from the mortgaged men
their smiles rustling in the sheets
pebbles washed up smooth on shore
black coral stolen from the reef
polished, pendant in a seller's box.
In a corner of her mind, childhood
sits on a broken stool gazing out
at star-shaped images spinning
stylish dances down the corridors
of the years. Not real. I, she says
for the first time, I also
made you unreal.

In this sun-curve of island
with bony spine of mountain
how does the boy grow real?
Real is dire warnings

De fruit neva fall far from de tree.
Father is someone, someplace else.
Used to get a Party work but
government change. Try a little hustle
with the weed, but Sergeant bustle him
straight into lockup. "You Honour,
do have mercy, is plenty pickney me have."

Five years, five years drop out
of a man's life, drop into blackness
and a stench and a state style
violence in government prison.
When I met him, fear, shame
sorrow all confused between us.
Father who never fathered me
forgive us our trespasses as we
forgive those whose eyes are
hollow, whose arms are empty
and anger in ropes of veins
collars his closed throat.

Real is seashore at daybreak
mountains filtering light on backs of men
pulling in the net, slow and steady
arm over arm, steady and slow
rope coiling smooth into sand.
We threw it out last evening under
clear skies that promised a good catch.

Slow and steady, net a dwindling arch
curling into shore. Empty.
Bucketful of frying sprats. Fine
blue morning in an empty net.
Ten silent men as sun-beat rises
fierce, drumming counterpoint
to the soft, mocking waves.

Curl up the net in boat
again set out to sea
again throw wide this net
of knotted hopes.

Only, Lord hear the prayers
of strong men, of men with muscle
and skill, with patience
honed sleek like silver fish,
of stubborn men
who cast their manhood daily
into the cold heart, salt wave
rocking of this master sea that gives
and gives not
in ways
we cannot fathom.

*   *   *

Island people, better is a far place where
loves, lives, years circle us like playful children
laughing under the sycamore trees,
hands out to catch the papery, winged seeds.
We are smiling, successful, degreed,
nestled softly in our homes in famous cities,
hablo espanol, *ich spreche Deutsches*,
waking slowly to ice-bright dreams.
But still we hear the whispers
Where are you coming from?
Where are you going?
Nowhere, nowhere.
Go home.

Coming back now I travel under
in time, in place, from the
nuzzling of sea on stone, those
intimate whispers that stir

the best dreams. Under,
mole blind, naked worm leaving
coiled, moist mounds, testing
texture of underground life,
the hum and busy zing of it, passing
old graves of softest dust.

Savage conquistadores
crumbled, crumbled.
Musket and pistol dead
beneath stale smell of pirates
flotsam and jetsam of Port Royal
crumbled, crumbled.

Low-life British of the slave yard,
their tiers of brothers, soldiers,
governors, syphilitic public servants
and their anxious, decaying wives
crumbled in a fine democracy of dust.
How lie the preachers, Lutherans, Moravians
building churches for a cool, correct God
'till the Baptists brought fire to the altar?

Stretching inland from the coast
into deep leaf-mould of forests
slave children curl little fists
round pungent ginger root,
their mothers plantations away
are polished bones under mango walks
where luscious fruit drop mocking
the dryness of their brief lives.
Where are the fathers, where are the fathers?
When the ginger blooms fragrant under
full moon, the children roam as birds,
as downy muted moths, as thoughts
of the past seeking their own.

This loss machetes through time, gleams
in eyes of that primary school boy, this
mobile, nubile university girl practising
her French — *Je n'ai jamais connu mon père* —
syntax, vocab chopped into silence.
Moi, je n'ai jamais connu ma mère.

Sandra, you do you homework?
Yes Auntie.
You wash you school uniform?
Yes Auntie.
You sweep up de yard?
Yes Auntie.

Auntie?
I can go picture show tomorrow?

Lord, you ever see my crosses.
You not goin all bout on de street.

Auntie I going to Regal with Blossom,
I not going anywhere else.

Chile, you keep yuself to yuself
an study yu books. Yu hear me?
Yes Auntie.
Is only edication can save poor people.
Yes Auntie.
Next ting is boyfriend foolishness
you coming wid.
No Auntie.

"Fire fire inna me wire, wire" —
bar music, dance hall, radio
night sounds pounding in
on every wavelength, bass notes

boom into her bed, throb
in the pit of her belly. Sandra
pretty little, can't sleep,
growing up girl.
    No man, yu not to do dat.
    Girl yu feel so sweet.

"Fire, fire inna me wire, wire"
Curled up tight, a drum beating
between her thighs, Sandra sighs,
wanting to love.
Scholarship girl, Auntie trying
so hard. Mama is a letter
now and again, a visit last year
with foreign clothes that can't fit.
But chile, with a Brooklyn accent,
how you grow so big?

I grew when you were in cold and
subway and factories and white
people homes, working the dollars
and the gold teeth and weave in
hair and I wanted to love you and
you to love me
and send for me
like you said
you would.

        All finished, all finished now.
        Under curling shingles, birds
        pick their way delicately through
        coiled brain; an arm, broken column
        on a distant hill, raises jagged
        edge of bone into a clouded sky.
        Dark corners of cellars hum
        with songs of horned beetles, and

windows staring out to sea draw
curtains of salt spray across
their tired eyes.

All finished now.
Find some other way to leave
the blind woman questioning.
Stop up the ears to cease
this listening, listening;
symphony of earth and stars,
of people and growing,
and always
the strong mountains
waiting, waiting
to claim their own.

PART IV

ORIGAMI

ORIGAMI

Time caught like flesh on a thorn —
dry mouth of sadness
but when it's all over
calm
soft fingers probe plumply
to my heart
peace
making space now memory
walks under trees —
slow drift of feet growing lichen-blue
shadows of trunks furring over
bark cracks, node scars
where twigs snapped as we scatter
drifting leaves in distant places.

When you write, a word, a pause
comes to me miles, months away.
Sweet breath
I fly always towards shadows
but when it's all over
I gather them
these white, drifting leaves,
these stars, swans, swallows —
paper spaces, origami of love.

GOING HOME

I should not have left.
Coming back my eyes are full of silt
but urged by the tolling bell
I swim up from dark waters
muddied with other cities.

I should have stayed
forever here in this cool church
hushed by the rustle of old ladies
so elegant their bone-thin faces
eyes outlined in perfect hollows
skins caramel pale with years.

Together since school days
and now, another funeral, one
more sister gone home to rest
under the cobalt gaze of Mary
and the saints' magenta robes
gone to her heavenly home
as they sing with tender, fragile voices
of life everlasting.

We should not have been allowed to leave;
our restless, brittle selves grow more foreign
with each passing year as we too age, alone
in distant cities, the drab cold days not ours
the rush and pull of speed not ours.
Here, this certainty of welcome
the blessing of these voices
pressed like flowers in a pew-worn bible
open up their songs of loss in my hot hand.

PORTLAND NIGHT

Scent of ginger lilies blooms up to meet
night flowing pearly-grey down rolling ridges,
massed mountains tucked in with wisps of mist.
Lilies and the nightingales singing, singing
trails of sweetness in the still trees.

Far below, turned on by the crie, crie
of tree frogs, lights firefly in the valley,
circle the harbour where the sea gleams
molten, heavy – the steady, powerful pulse
of this sleeping island.

In this room, a fan whispers, soft
counterpoint to your quiet breath
drifting smooth into smiling sleep.
Small human, this heart soars
singing the stars into place.

FOR JEAN

Moonlight brings my sister
breathless with talk; laughing,
she lights a cigarette, stories swirl
in smoke, the miles between us
melted in this dream reunion.

My lover, honeyed nonchalance,
slips in on moon tide, lovely
man, to lie in my chaste bed,
ruffling it with memories; sheets,
sighs, smiles slipping from us.

Daylight takes my ghosts
as sun on leaves sparkle
in a smile, a glass of wine.
My friend feeds me lunch,
a bunch of all-shades red
flowers glowing on the table.

I feel my father's death and tears
threaten under whispered prayers
for far loves. At that table
grace turns me gently with her
wings; give thanks for the glory
of a good friend in the real
red-petalled light of today.

DECEMBER EVENING

December evening.
Something in the air
in a red rose given; something
is going to happen. What? Who?
A visitor from a past life, mists,
ancient mysteries unfolding through
a chance remark blown in from the street,
a book picked up at random through which
the scent of lemons, burnished rinds
of tangerines bring whispers of a place,
whorls of memories leaving trails
of restless pleasure on a quiet evening.

The end of the year
weighs us down, a flat lake
shrouding the brain, body,
grey webs of languor, ennui.
In cities far away bare trees
hang sketchily in the dusk.
A fire casts its glow where
someone is reading. Here
the glow of a December evening
showers gold on the garden, turning
simple leaves into amber pendants
nestling at the throat of the day.

The moon and the year
are waning. Inauspicious signs.
Yet dawn shows green shoots
beside amputated banana stumps.
Sorrel and gungo hang gossiping
over the fence and a rose,
inexpertly pruned, hides a bud,
baby-fisted, in curled, new leaves.

FROM PINEGROVE

Driven, driven to embrace the difficult
as the puritan ethic rattles its dry cough,
ease, pleasure are for the idle.
Yet, give me this one hour
over and over again:
riding into the hills,
stepping out on a wide verandah
to hang in a free space ringed
with great archways of mountains.
Gold glimmers on a slope where
the setting sun lingers
a hushed parting.
Others stretch deep-blue greenness
into the wine-dark sky,
yet others wrap their heights
in purple, rich royal promise:
Nirvana
lies
in the sweep of an eye,
rests
in the beat of a heart.

PRAISESONG FOR DENNIS

Remember?
Beach in moonlight and friends
drinking cider from the winner's cup
of your first play,
barefoot dreamers on the sand,
all the world so young, so open
for us, and the sea
whispering and curling
up the arches of our feet.

These hills stand round knowing you
had never left but carried them
folded round and round your heart.
These streets empty at evening
knew you would come, soft cat's step
up to the doors of our lives,
energy man and secret smiling
as the music flames and flowers
behind your sheltered eyes.

Caught in covers we named them poems
but still they dance, fluttering at mind's edge.
On sudden restless waking, shh... hear them
tap... tapping... come and play, and weep
sometimes and laugh and catch your breath
at the sharp, fierce light of them, for here
this bird is free and will fly for you.

Singing still for so many
accept: the notes of this song are
young feet at water's edge, leaves rustling
and bleached bone and honey on the tongue,
salt taste of tears and loving
in all its paths, and that you gave us

all this and
the wings of your dream

give thanks.

Dennis Scott, Jamaican poet and playwright

TEATIME

Panes of glass shelter
gossamer china lest they escape,
fly away – brittle handles caught
on cactus, fluted rims singing
past rutted country roads
whose stones, now groomed, polished,
catch sun-sparkles through
manorial doors expansively open.
Toast with English jam from
crystal bowl delicate as angel tears,
while vandas hang their purple heads
penitent over framed photos,
their café-au-lait subjects
slightly sporty, slightly kennedy –
this borrowed gentility
of our light-skinned aristocrats.

Imposter at all levels
I know which knife for fruit,
which for jam. I know
the silent tread of Pam,
black housemaid on calloused feet.
More tea, a scone perhaps.
I know nothing. Brief guest,
my spirit shrinks, grows dark
in this gleaming room.

FOR ISABEL ALLENDE

I love your books
characters floating out
my room smells of winter
city streets and damp mountains,
apricots, smooth skin of lovers
and the sudden beauty of truth.

Guns in the street here
death in narrow lanes
crouched western style
behind zinc fences
and the children
watching
learning.

I hide away from it
lost in your world –
a fine art that to make
love in death.

Shaping here a story
but wordless for love
the fiction curls, dark moths
caught in scattered fires
flame briefly
float away in smoke
over the trembling city.

THE GIFT

A stranger tells me
over party platters, pale
shrimp crescents tenderly veined
over ice melting in washed-out rum,
of a church in Italy.

In a warm Jamaican night
the ladies come and go
talking of Michael and Angelo.

A church in Italy, evening
wraps her throat in silken scarves
a quartet plays Mozart.

Does it go to God
this perfection of sound?
Does it go to that
perfection of silence?

Quickly given, he moves away.
It takes root there, flowers into
nave, worn pews, a Madonna
with sky-blue cape
and the violin rising rafter high.

Does he have it still, the church,
distant smell of tomatoes, basil strewn,
and fever touch of red wine,
does he have it still?

My Madonna opens wide her arms,
a pale night rain falls
washed thin silver by the flute,
and the cello moans
softly, softly.

MOZART AT THE MAYFLOWER HOTEL – IOWA

Mozart sets sail
out into autumn trees
the dream catchers
their branches webs of summer fading
through which a flight of birds draws
winter with one charcoal stroke.
Stillness
thoughts turn free
leaves in a pale sky
closed in warm room of notes
fall as flow on paper
a life-score wrapped
safe in sound.

THAT LAST DAY

Like charred paper fleeing
a bonfire, starlings flicker home.

One red bird, high priest
of winter lights in black branches,
echo of their fiery glory
so tender the drifting snow.

Now time to go, I linger,
faithless lover, my island heart
seduced by winter magic.

Dark night, a star, sickle moon cupped
symbol for a map not mine.
Where to make a life?
At strange doors
by shaded windows
in empty rooms?

The moon waxes and wanes
yet keeps a steady path

So sketch a new terrain
with signposts of old loves
move on to new summers
moons full over leafy trees.

In this winter room
faith is a small hand
closing the case
opening the door.

FOR IMBUGA, KOBENA AND MOYEZ

I had thought the diaspora, this wrenching
of people, this whip of suffering in ship's belly,
was a livid scar on the back of God's hand.

Kobena's voice is the roar of thunder, and
the deep, rich tones of Imbuga rise up
like daybreak, spread across the mountains
and Moyez says his truths in laughter.

Listening there to my brothers from Africa
light pours into my heart. I see that God
put her hands deep in the earth of Africa,
scooped out two handfuls and threw us in
two shining arcs, one from North to South America
and she said:

> My children, learn the alphabet
> of these wide plains, these deep
> rivers of the two Americas;

and she opened her other hand and threw
us wide in a sparkling crescent
into the Caribbean and she said:

> My children, learn the truth
> of these islands that are
> my personal adornment, pure jewels
> of beauty that nestle at my throat
> close to the seat of my voice
> where all songs have their beginning.

When it was done, she knelt once more
and from the fragrance of India sprinkled
a dusting of this ancient race, like sweet

herbs to season our understanding, into the
heart of Africa, into the soul of the islands,
and she said:

> *My children, learn that the East*
> *and the West flow together in*
> *my veins, are plaited close in the*
> *sweet blackness of my hair.*

Not knowing the wonders of this thing
we threw ourselves into a new wandering
in silver birds, on iron railroad tracks
we made a new wave, leaving the South
flying like birds from the islands
we clipped our own wings and fell
crowded into the belly of a new slavery
the great white cities of the North.

This spreading out I saw as a sadness
as a weakness, as a path to homelessness
far from our own. But now I put my ear
close to the heart of our poets
and their voices are all the drums
and all the instruments of air
of strings, of deep-throated horns,
and the harmony is a net knotted
and thrown wide, and this is a faith
and this is a future and this is a
great shining song of possibilities.

Francis Imbuga: playwright, Kenya; Kobena Acqua, poet, Ghana; Moyez
Vassanji, novelist, Tanzania

PART V

FLORIDA BLUES

FLORIDA BLUES

This sumptuous restaurant, transported Italiano,
was once cow pasture, spirits of the ancestors
paved over for creamy cannelloni, garlicky
broccoli sprouting from ancient cow pats.
Two years ago that mall was tall trees
bulldozed for K-Mart; a bald eagle's nest
crashed, churned under and put your ear
here to the wall of this Eckerds or that
pastel Burdines and hear his regal screams.

Sing a song of subdivisions, finger-tip
towels and designer toilet paper; praise
the electronic garages, power tool stacked;
add an aria for the one tree out back, the
hand-gun in the colour-coded linen closet,
one more chorus for the neatness of lives
snug in king-size beds; for decaffeinated,
natural, lite, no cholesterol, microwave kitchens.

Yet exit here and find a shaded place,
grackles gleam indigo blue up from reeds
waving at lake edge, red wing blackbirds
flash in flight homeward as the sun drifts
down behind the melancholy call of coots.
Flushed sunset spreads a warm benediction
between the plutonium sky at Space Coast and
the deep green lawns of orderly retirement homes.
Florida gasps for breath in small corners
under the moss-weeping trees and warm swamp
breath of this threatened, tenacious landscape.

LAUDERDALE-BY-THE-SEA

Paradise by the Sea
floats slightly, rocks this way and that
to the steady beat of the rain,
grey, like old men's voices
washing sibilant over the split, splat
of their evening card game.

Bright balloons anchored in primary colours
on the *Mardi Gras Motel* sign next door
seem to slip, wash down to the street
lighting a tree shaded puddle red
and green and falsely bright
sunshine-yellow.

A man and woman run in laughing
he brushes water from her hair.
Caught in the splash and shimmer
of the *Mardi Gras Motel*, in this damp
here and now shine, they glow
pleased with themselves
for being in love.

KEY WEST

All the way there, the men
outlined against the shadowless sun
cast for fish, and the women, the children,
solitary or in small familial knots, cast their lines
dark exclamation marks punctuating the
still, unbroken sea, buckets of bait
at their steady, planted feet.

The beauty of it, these age-old images
of human stillness, of languid but focused intent
as the Keys trail pointed fingers at Cuba
at the Bahamas, the islands nuzzled close
but separate, to the end of American life.

This long road with its tonsure of stunted trees
its scattered white herons keeping watch
in the empty church of a domed blue sky,
brown pelicans, homely parishioners,
diving for wafers of silvered fish, is a dream
a pause in Florida's last glimpse of itself
before the sudden bustle of the town, the last
hurried grasp of dollars and suntans and tart
lemonades sipped at cool cafes where waiters
hover like hummingbirds in the humid air.

Ice cream scoops of pastel houses, their
fretwork trim so crisp, like lace doilies at
afternoon tea, the gardens leafy, overgrown,
inviting hidden meetings, sudden touch of lips
against lips, hand against cheek, before poincianas
shed their full red light, petals flaming briefly
at these careless, holiday feet.

MALLORY SQUARE – KEY WEST

The sun fell into the sea
at the end of America. No flags,
soldiers, no bugle-call of Taps
but a Scots man playing a bagpipe,
a bride and groom, magazine romantic,
waving from a sailing ship and in
Mallory Square at the end of America
we stare at the sun, at the sea, at the
picture-book couple sailing into the sunset.

A man with bad teeth swallows a sword,
another juggles a flaming stick
around his waist. "Oh mind your jewels!"
gasps a woman, her happy hour flush
bright over a paper cup of vodka.
An Indian woman sells woven bracelets,
a Rasta man beats a drum, two rail-thin women
with dyed hair embrace tenderly, and the
tourists, fleeing their nightmare of fluorescent
work stations, their anxious sales targets or
their stand-on-the-feet-all-day-in-the-store jobs,
laugh in the golden sun-silk light
at the end of America
or at her beginning.

CODA

What do you know, old woman?
I know nothing. My mind is an empty
begging bowl turned up to the sun.

What do you know, old woman?
The sun courses through my fingers
pools sparkling at my naked feet.
How sweet it is to walk in the light!

Standing in a clear, cold river
stones smooth on the balls of my toes,
strength of the river flowing in my bones –
ten, thirty, fifty years, it's all the same
I am still seeking.

I am whittled down sleek as a flute
senses honed fine and free.
I see less but the details stop my breath
I hear less but the notes fall bright as rain
into my heart.

This is all I have
all that beats in my veins
to seek, to walk, to lift up hands
to touch each dazzling note
all things bright and beautiful.

QUADRILLE FOR TIGERS
(1984)

Sweeping an arc over
she rakes almond leaves,
rustling pile of thinness.
A simple mantra
grows in the dust.

NAUTILUS

Hesitantly, the smoky blue flower
cranium-wrapped blooms open,
fluting through parted lashes of
hidden eyes, prisms of sound,
deep shaft to waken
old goddesses,
long silent icons.

Moon pearls fused together
smoothed a vault for the sea,
a cradle for wet light. Curled
in the hidden beginning a promise,
growth is given slowly, unannounced.
In time, calm water, a perfect
nautilus in the hand.

THE LIGHT

My bamboo cage turns
splitting trapped light;
louvres fold inward
brittle shade blocked in.
Such attempts at order
under a too wide sky.

Zen, Onyame, Jah.
Yet how to turn from
acts of making, breaking:
accept stillness, welcome silence.

Strips of bamboo curve
inward, meet at
beginning and completing.
Dark, light are shadows
for each other. A small
energy, heat makes movement
in quiet arcs. So it is
making and acceptance.

FOR D.S.

Once the stone god turned its
marble eyes and breathed out
moonlit fire on my thoughts.
Once I saw a river born, thrown
free from veins of chalky earth.
Once I even saw an egret,
white throat stretched, swallow
the sunset all in one gulp.

But once, behind your sheltered eyes
I saw a flower curving from your palm.

LOST FROM THE FOLD

Lost from the fold.
Can't believe in
His infinite mercy
when I see a woman,
age uncertain, legs
like gaulins, but crumpled
across the gutter.
Death, the certain friend
but he lingers, takes
his time, scuffling his adidas,
breaking off a piece of macka
to pick his teeth.

Where is the dove, the lamb
those feathered and fleecy
pets of her Sunday school?
Where the noble lion
of Judah to bear Jah's
daughter home? Where, here
Death the certain friend
come to stun her with
the sun of this hell
while his dread friend
Hunger skanks in her
shrivelled belly.

Gaulins: Egrets – elegant, slender necked white birds with long spindly legs
Macka: a long thorn
Skanks: a kind of dance, also young street males who live by their wits

DROUGHT

Sliver of river
trickle of wet
enter my body,
lush me up
green me up,
pour liquid and growing
round my dry frame.

Build dams to hold back
dusty dreams and thoughts;
paint instead a shining sky of stars,
gold plains and cobalt mountains
alive in my flesh.

NEW YEAR

The new year comes to meet us
wrapped in a gleaming cloak
of silver rain. All the obtuse
divisive words seem hollow now.
Wet leaves, white blossoms
quiver a tremulous clarity,
liquid mirror of today's truth.

No tears for this aging lover,
our feet turn towards young hands,
young, warm hands along our backs,
our eyes brimming with green and wet.
In the still heart of our hills
a stream grows full with itself,
hugging into its curves slender grasses.

For just a little longer we straddle
the thin meridian, roll around the tongue
an ashy taste of what has gone, yet
part our lips for what is to come.

Hurry away old man with bitter eyes,
the rain takes your footprints
before they are made. This year
you did not take away the curve
from my child's body; for that
I give thanks.
We will take growing and singing with us
into the quiet rain.

PRELUDE TO ANOTHER LIFE

My grandfather, Sarah's husband,
courted her for fifteen years. Not
to be imagined in these days of haste.
The not-to-be-had lover sailed to Africa
and taught in missionary school.
Lost to time his continental thoughts,
but he returned and pressed his suit
again. Well, yes, she would walk out
with him. In his zeal he built a house,
smoothed the furniture himself, till at last
she plumped into the nest.

They lived mostly on what they grew.
All around them spread the red lands.
Land and church. Grandmother took in
other children to pupil teach as her
brood grew to four. Shaped and planed
them all for scholarship class.
A dose of salts before exams to clear
the head and in they flew through
the sacred gates of secondary education.

Sarah Gertrude, I hear you were a tartar
of ambition, but I knew you as the keeper
of a bookcase full of dark bindings
and faded gold titles. Most had only print
but some had children with hoops and
lace-edged bloomers about their ankles.
I knew you playing songs of robins and
linnets and gentle jesus on the piano
under a hissing gas lamp and a marble
lady only half clothed. She was Hope,
I think, and on her snowy bosom
many a fluted moth dashed to death
under the sibilant lamp and too-ra-loos.

Grandfather, silent in the nest,
taught us outside the names of trees.
Mahogany and cedar, not to be confused
with bastard cedar, though she was
accepted, in her own way. I loved
the bouncy cashew limbs but stayed
away from yellow logwood where
bees clustered treacherously golden.

My sister Penelope Ann
was small and slim as a can
of oil kept for the Singer.
Her hair was long and black;
Louise the cook brushed and crooned
Ah, I love this coolie one.
Twins, yet I was pale
with red curls. Unfair
not to be dark
with long, black hair;
despair.

Older sister went to boarding school.
Dimly known, her freckled plumpness
but guessed at, this older genius
who could write proper letters
with a stamp. Fetched from
the post office on donkey back,
oh the foreign crispness
of that letter sent all the way
from Brown's Town, distant
to us as Grandfather's tales
of Orion and the Milky Way.

In the envelope she had tucked
a picture each, a butterfly,
a flower, glorious in crayon colours.

So marvelled at these proofs of
older prowess while we thumped
"Frere Jacques" on the piano and
learned to read and write, recite
tales of frogs a-wooing and daffodils.

We grew up with bowels
well regulated by fear
of the pit latrine at night,
where flopping bull-frogs lurked.
Our bath was a large, tin tub
set out at midday to heat, then
dragged inside so we might wash
our five-year-old skins
in gloomy modesty.

What was there in that
courtyard that might see
our twin delights? A large
mesh-covered tank, a smoky
outhouse hung with tobacco leaves
and all beyond, flat fruited land.
No rows of prying eyes, only cassava
sticks stacked for planting.

Yet were we bundled into clothes
and in the house properly cared
as children over whom the golden E
might one day shine. But in the yard,
far from adult eyes, we swung like monkeys
from limb to limb or hung upside down
watching land and sky swing towards
a strange embrace.

Once, saddened that our father
did not come to take us for a
long awaited picnic to the sea,
we stripped and leapt into the duck pond.
Gaily splashing in the greeny slime,
the forbidden and the blissful
came to be one and the same, for
we were snatched angrily from this
naked ooze and scrubbed in a tub
full of herbs to ward off scabies,
ringworm and the sin of disobedience.

Grandfather was a lay preacher.
Grandmother kept Sunday School.
Sunday was one long and silent
whiteness as we learned our collect
and waited through two services for lunch.
Yet I liked the scooping hymns and
little pictures given out of a long-haired
Jesus in a bathrobe surrounded by
angelic children. Knowing no long-haired
skirted men we clasped the pictures
for they fuelled our belief that
the world was strange and wonderful.

Abruptly hauled into the city
to start another life, for us
all harmony, all innocence
was left behind in the red lands.
Gradually the real grandmother
became fused with a portrait
of a young Sarah, straight back,
waspish waist, edited expression
but a head of hair so thick and lively
it betrayed the other trappings of propriety.

Uprooted from my own past
I invented for her an inner past
and seemed to sit there in her dreaming
as she paused in her pupil teaching,
dipped quick in the Quink, and caught
a glimpse of sunny morning laid outside
the door. Not much time to dream
for she could only see dust and
deep anxiety for those without
the golden hope of education.
Through a sea of khaki and starched
navy in the one-roomed parish school
she transmuted her own dreams and fears
into lively learning.

The red lands, at once
her prison and her love,
sold now and mined for bauxite;
those plains where Grandfather
rode as agricultural inspector
upturned by giant forks;
those homes of postcard blue and pink
ringed with whitewashed stones
replaced by concrete palaces
flush toilets, *Time*, *Readers Digest*
and posturpedic springs.
What was glimpsed through art
what was real through time,
these remain the adult shadows,
golden bridges of our twinned childhood.

CROW POEM

I want so much to put
my arms around you but
extended they are feathered
vanes, snapped, tatty things
no longer curving.

My voice wants to say things
about blue skies, blond sand,
yet a rasping, carrion croak
jets from my beak
sharp edged.

Condemned to live a life for which
I am ill suited, improperly
dressed. Perhaps there is out there
one crow, wheeling over the city dump,
convinced she is a woman.

ST. ANN

Capture for me
all the quiet of this country day.
Hills stand softly at the edge of
small dreaming farms.
Furled pumpkin leaves
lie drooped towards
the hot earth.

So many noisy leaves
clashing reds and yellows seem
muted in this silent heat.
Under an ancient guango
cows abandon fly-swishing sleep.

Guango: large, symmetrical spreading shade tree

LEAF

Brown, black and grey, spoked.
She laid it on a white formica table
beside a plastic vase with paper roses.
"See this leaf," she said. "Wow!"

She was busy, a flash in water
splashing silvered limbs, eyes
briefly pearled with drops that
melted with the larger flow to form
again on fingers, lobes of ears.

At night, with little protests,
her sunburnt back slim between
pink polyester sheets, she slept.
Such a small breathing in the dark.

It closed upon itself then
darker, smaller, drew its ribs
into a crumpled furl. Table,
vapid factory vase stood vigil
unmoved by this brief life.

DAYS WHEN DEMONS

Days when the demons
flap their feathered fins,
how heavy my already heavy
eyes.

Peer through shiny leaves
dust settles beneath them;
float a blossom in the palm and
sigh.

The henna bush blooms golden
yet red comes from it;
the grass is deep but my feet are
dry.

The Tao says, "Shape clay into a vessel;
it is the space within that makes it useful."
So this heart beats life but is empty.
Why?

MR. BROWN AND MRS. SMITH

Lusting quietly for all that brown
the puritan sits, legs crossed
at the ankles. Out of her mouth
words bloom, reasoned discussion,
ironic, self mocking.
In her own landscape the brush
grows quickly, she knows.

Hot lady whore is a gardener
sitting in the corner of her eyes
waiting to prune and bloom,
watching, noting the little pulse
alive in his neck.

The brown watches, laughing,
dishing out just enough help
to both to set them clawing
in her hips. The ankles win;
they have had more practice.

Thirsty miss whore sighs as
the hedge grows higher.
The brown only smiles.
He will not open the gate
for her; he won't quite
close it either.

When a breeze
rustles through the bamboo
the sound is louder
in its going.

POEM FOR A MARRIAGE

My love, I learned
to trim the branches
of my fears for you.
Now I sense your lifting
slightly your protective shell
for me.

It was such a glorious, shapely shell,
comforting, cool inside.
But even when the day is harsh
I love the sun. I will bare
my face, throw wide my arms
and love you more on the open plain.

MRS. JONES

Flat bed of sand
strewn with the boulders
of his will.
A death heat, sharp,
draws squares
in the sand.
In a corner, she shivers,
turns away
for the last time now.
For in her head lilies bloom
muskrose, stars and ancient heroes.

STORM – JAMAICA

The morning had been quiet.
Little tongues of sunlight stammered
through the garden praising now
a yellow bell, now a mauve bauhinia,
rattling brown seed cases which hung
beneath those few flowers still
clinging, pale ovary inside calyx,
when time had since converted
other sisters to parchment pods.

At midday the sun set behind
a sheet of sky sent grey from
the laundry instead of Sudsil white.
Mother fetched her own inside, clothes,
children bundled behind shut panes.
Father, weary, gave himself a nap
but short, for the zinging round
his head of flying demons.

We waited. Great Wagnerian
rolls of thunder spread unchallenged,
strings, flutes had all laid back
to some dark dumbness. Through the
wooden fretwork we half-peered
for fireworks. Strange, no flash, no light,
only a heaving grey of sound.

Evening came before it. Our nerves
sizzled in the dusk. Little spats
of temper burst through supper,
healed, escaped again. Faults noted,
brick on brick a castle of disorder.

In time this wretched day will be dissolved.
Small living habits, efforts at loving
will clear the windows. But those lofty arches
we had dreamt are still mud bricks,
this inward rusty zinc more firm than they.

THE CAUSEWAY

On one side, white buildings,
unicolour lego lining the port,
grasping in cold storage goods
export earnings, import quotas,
a column of figures for the bank.

On the other, small white boxes
holding frail families. Trim
gardens, picket fences and other
walled assurances of progress,
which is what we are about – yes?

Through the middle a black stretch,
varying heights of corporate entrails
openly rotting or wreathed in caustic
smoke. There black men, grey-skinned,
probe, push, pull out the city's excreta
with a stunning sense of purpose.

Not far away, in a white hall
we listen as our poets sculpt
our stifling days, spark new planets
in a sky we had thought far, bleak.
One young poet speaks, a song
muffled in smoke. We are helpless;
he trembles, crossing his own causeway.

TWO PEOPLE

There are two people living uneasily
in this house. One says life is rational,
there are plans to be made, work to be done.
Be happy that the sun rises in the morning,
leaps away in a burst of fire
only to rise again the next.
The other says, life is the crazy
whirling baton of some cosmic conductor.
As soon as you grasp the score it shifts
key. The well-tuned flute at your lips
is useless for these new, discordant themes.

These two, trying to make one song,
one note even, to unbend the twisted
tree, polish open/closed faces,
one sound so pure the pulse would
beat and stop and beat again.
But lost in tones and minor keys,
unbalanced she says, a pagan god
spat on my birthday, I am lost.

Well hear me now. I will defy
you all, smash your baton,
cover your spit with earth.
In the blackness of night
in the softness of dreams
I will find a gust of air,
fill my lungs loud, loud with laughter
to shout my song.

Her freckled plumpness wedged
in school, all things bright and
beautiful with early morning care,
drink your juice, you not going anywhere
in those dirty shoes. Her face sad
just at the edges. Sometimes she says
it gets to her. She wants to stay home.

Eyes mussed with tears
fumbling for the gears
in grinding traffic I feel
disaster in every nerve.
Yesterday, a silent crowd, still
as the law cracked open the boy's face.
Today, children at traffic lights
with a rock, with a shining
jagged bottle, blood in the mouth,
and a crowd in cars moving on.

This city of silence where
children have their humanity
beaten out or trodden down.
Women's lives shot to stillness
in small, hot rooms. Men
bought and sold, holding death bold
in the gleam of guns,
a deadly phallic power against
the impotence of poverty.

In the face of this heavy terror
the mothers polish and shine, starch
and press the children into school.
They must be safe, warm in the magic
of routine. Any job is better than none,

so the school fees can pay, so the money
can stretch for more school books.

Where the roads and words divide us,
where the men prey upon us and lay
upon us their hollow version of
the hunter myth, or reveal a
small tenderness, quickly hid,
still we wake as one each day,
pull out the treasures of our life
to bank them neat in school.
One steady act of hope, one heart
one love, safe in the mother faith.

WITHOUT APOLOGY TO PROUST

A sleeping girl
holds in a circle
around her

All the backyards, zincky fences
flattened to a smooth path
for Sheba and Nanny riding
laughing through her cells.

In the sweet heat of her veins
Erzulie, Diana step smooth
on a carpet of mint spread from
her back-step pot, always tended.

A sleeping girl
holds
in a circle

daily dispersed grains of
possible, made one smooth shell
for her quiet ear. Rolling of waves,
flowing of deep rivers in her time.

Nanny: a Maroon leader and one of Jamaica's national heroes.

THE MOTHERLESS ONES

The motherless ones
sail frail canoes,
oars swishing, churn
deep seas, the smallest wave
a threat.
Floating far off and a cry
mingled with the sea gulls' hoot.

Do you hear, you hear
the child in the shell
seaweed soft, cradle this
hold this tender mollusc,
shape a head and eyes
give arms and strong feet.
Aieee… trembles and is still.

The others wear shiny dresses
to match patent shoes and socks
and blowing candles and happy birthdays.
Far off, the motherless ones stalk
the shores, years like footprints wash
behind them. The adult rubs an eye,
makes another craft to hold steady
sail for this endless journey.

IN THE FRILLS OF JACARANDA

In the frills of jacaranda
little girls are stepping lightly,
slim through squares of glassy colour
beaming into frowsty church.

In the spills of alamanda
young men coiling out at dusk
see the dragons of their future
melted in their softened lust.

Ah the red of poinciana
hopes of mamas lost in trust,
sweaty preacher coins in sadness
dries those petals dark as moths.

Looking forward to seeing
you as the poui spreads
a golden scarf in your honour.

                                        Four girls on a yellow carpet
                                        dark legs soft under
                                        the stand of poui.

Poui: (*tabebuia*) Yellow flowering tree whose blossoms have a short-
lived, breathtaking beauty.

NOMMO

Moonlight, midnight melodrama.
Hooded, faceless crone
strikes across a dream
suffocating, the odorless
speechless weight of her will.

Nommo, I want sounds
to pound the dark weight
of this silence and words
to halt the creep of her feet,
and songs to be flung
in the lanes, in the street
and heart not to catch
in the pause, in the cold
of her beat.

LOVE POEM

Seeing you walking then
hip lifting slightly on the left,
arm swinging out in an unfinished circle,
I considered your body so finite
so clothed away from me
and neat ended in laced-up shoes
that I wanted urgently, then
and at that time
to step across the sun-daubed
peopled pavement
and make a small, dark space
for us.

FOR THE SAX PLAYER

clear music spiral — sound in flight
aztec birds swift through early forests,
stream moving heavy, spreckled gold
molten subterranean metals.
i hear you man
calling out through space and time
rich, rich gift blowing out the soul
high and wide, sweet travel
mind in flight
swirling lucid tones
so near to
the center
man you give me happiness
for pure whole measures
of liquid time.

FOR EDNA MANLEY

Silvered lady
your reflection traced
on so many outstretched
hands which curling
back upon themselves
found their own dreams
in a magic splash
spinning out on paper,
canvas, chipped from stone.

How many times
gleaming lady
did you throw your tides wide
and in some special feel of time
gather them close again,
leaving your young loves
full of a spangled belief
in the hopes they could
fashion into a moving future.

You should laugh,
all this fancy! Fern,
moon, muse, what are these
when still an arc of light
spins from your fingers
making grained wood, stone
shiver into living forms?
What else matters but this life
grown from a wild, loving landscape?

DREAM I

Sliding, slipping on the zinc roof
dream picks her way, fastidious
not to make a tear in the mind
that formed her. Drumming lightly
with polished balls of toes, balance,
springs off his cortex, one finger
soft on cerebellum in passing.
Zinc, bone give way.

Once she stayed for days, heating
his eyes fixed on ripening corn.
Gold in his hands, gold in his head,
till the drought, hot, hot zinc.
Hard to keep her now.

DREAM II

Dream heavy with fear
dull demons in every day
dress, some wire-meshed, some
dropping over walls, slime
deep eyes wormed with hate.

Yet, days so freshly sparkling
yellow satin cups, green growing up
eludes all imposed care. One area
chopped lies in browning waves;
still some stubborn tops remain
tri-forked in nesty clumps
making a nursery
for fragile butterflies.

Night seems far away as Mars.
nothing lurks in the brilliant garden,
cleared arena for quick human pleasures.
Laugh more loudly, speak more firmly
in this perfect garden of days.

Sudden meetings, jewelled in the eye
of possibility, flash through sun,
mountains of this known world, but
so quickly as the light slips out
dissolve to other places
bridged by hollow echoes of questions.
Each goodbye now a loss of day.

FOR AUDREY

I kept making this dress every year.
I know it was a little limited, a trifle
dowdy, yet it had a certain elegance.
Laughing, you held my grey dress,
bringing instead armfuls of
pink frills, black satin, red lace.
They are all you, you said,
wear them, wear them now.

Quick in other ways, I've been
slow to come out of my tunnel,
but I am going to surface. And you,
what can I give you? I have nothing
tangible, nothing brought from a surly
shopgirl, disguised in shiny paper.
Only the shawl of our friendship
woven in hours of laughter and talk,
patterned with a little anger
and some tears.

Take it with you on the days
brimming over with good things.
Wear it in the nights crowded
with bright moons and stars.
On those few days when the wind
creeps under the door
draw it close around you.

LOLA THE HEAVENLY SINNER

On the good nights Lola dreams
Lucy in the sky with diamonds.
In the bad nights she remembers
I love you child, say you're sorry.
The Lord your God is a Jealous God
Repent and Conform.
You are my woman.

In her small house up under
moon's crag Lola cries, whispers
I repent, I am sorry. What have I done?
Original sin. Spread out in genes,
chromosomes, licking lasciviously through
capillaries, running unfettered through veins.
I am. Lola you are.

In the Indian jungles peter-pan-
collared American men broke,
splintered the great external forces.
Believe now that sin is in you.
Planting their gardens
cleaning their houses
their strange clothes on our breasts,
we believe.

Lola Lola I want
Lola let me just
Lola touch me there
It is done.

Sss… sss… sssh… I am
You are, you sin.

In her room by the water's edge
Lola lies on the floor sweltering
under four layers, yet the nape
is naked. Naked skin. Cover
a long scarf round and round her
naked neck, tighten the rasping
scream, blot up the stream of water
that cannot wash.

SUNDAY IN THE LANE

Every Sunday in the lane
church heavies the gentle air.
Every Sunday in the lane
someone beats a child.
Over the syrup of *Praise the Lord*
comes a cry, sobs tearing across
the yards and dusty trees.

Every Saturday in the lane
Comes the rub a dub of sounds,
Reggae, Motown, a giant broom
to sweep away the week's worries.
The clothes that can't wash for the
taps dry. The rent that can't pay
for the money no nuff. The man
that swearing you down sake of he
have a little young gal on the side.

Comes Sunday, smoke of burning
rubbish starts the morning. Dirt
all banished before a whiff, a
teasing hint of Sunday dinner
can find its spicy liberation. A lull,
then the Lord comes down in radio glory
and someone beats a child.
Chastisement and Church,
Sunday brothers
in the lane.

QUADRILLE, FOR TIGERS

In all your straight lines
I curve trying to find
a little hollow
a gap under the window
through which to climb
into your friendship.

On the cool slope
of white hibiscus
a humming bird
shakes his emerald glow
and sits, small head tilted.
How easy his poise,
how sweet their stillness.

In the streets and broken houses
we put our thorns first.
Harsh words roll along the cracks,
harsher thoughts drip from reddened eyes
as every day we turn a knife
between our apathy and anger.

Between the noise and silence
we move in careful steps
each with too much past unsorted
for brisker measure. But I am weary
of this slow quadrille, for tigers
leap behind my clouded brain
spiders stretch their furry joints
ready to trip me out of step.

FOR KLAUS OR JOHN OR PIERRE

Here's how it is, blond man staring.
Your eyes shout out across the black
faces. I can't know why you chose
to do penance here but we'll
make you pay, in silence,
politeness and a great distance.
History lays a hand on us, stronger
than school rules and prefects
and fear of wearing the wrong uniform
on the right day. Other people's hotly
catalogued experience races across
the shade-spattered lawn, writing
a law more binding than your gaze.

One thing we had in common,
when you were five, dreaming
over an open atlas, when I was
five, queen of the backyard
we didn't know that being adult
meant
more steps and gates
and latches on gates
and shiny pictures
not to be touched,
drawers with ornate clasps
not to be opened.

THE CHAIN

I no longer care, keeping close my silence
has been a weight,
a lever pressing out my mind.
I want it told and said and printed down
the dry gullies,
circled through the muddy pools
outside my door.
I want it sung out high by thin-voiced elders,
front-rowing murky churches.
I want it known by grey faces queuing under
greyer skies in countries waking
and sleeping with sleet and fog.
I want it known by hot faces pressed against
dust streaked windows of country buses.

    And you must know this now,
    I, me, I am a free black woman.
    My grandmothers and their mothers
    knew this and kept their silence
    to compost up their strength,
    kept it hidden
    and played the game of deference
    and agreement and pliant will.

It must be known now how that silent legacy
nourished and infused such a line,
such a close linked chain
to hold us until we could speak
until we could speak out
loud enough to hear ourselves
loud enough to hear ourselves
and believe our own words.

I AM A GYMNAST

I am a gymnast
see me fly and curve
see my arms stretched
my legs flexed to leap.

When the work goes badly
poise, balance, desert me utterly.
Crouched on my mat all day
I breathe in gritty dust.

SCARLATTI

And now I hate Scarlatti.
In that bare room, no soft seats
to cushion the sound, no warm surfaces
of cloth or wood, all organic life
denied this empty house, only the sound,
note after note a rain of icy crystal
in the heart, in the brain. Another
and I waiting with Scarlatti for your return.

It is morning now. In my house, alone,
the wind sweeps round, blowing small curled
leaves through the open windows. The play
of light through every door more splendid
than a thousand notes of human song. And you,
making yourself upon a barren, loveless image,
are far from me and this perfection of a day.

 Ah my love, what is more desolate than loveless
 lovers? What more bitter than the knowing
 it need not be?
 The wrong score has us meeting when you
 are throwing out all growing things
 while I upon the black cliffs of your heart
 stretch out for sun and wind and budding trees.

And now I hate Scarlatti
hate those cold notes of one man's genius.
If you should ever hold your heart in stillness
or for one moment
touch the warm place
where sun on bark of tree has lain,
come to my quiet house where I wait.

Harsh to go now
when the garden blooms deep
round the house that was ours.

CURLED IN THE LONG VALLEY

Curled in the long valley
of your back I knew your spirit
like a panther, lithe, treacherous
and I who would speak a thousand words
was dumb with the fear of that knowing.
From that dark, sinuous cave
where we had briefly locked reality
into a silent, whirling lake
I struggled to free myself.
In my going, I would celebrate you,
remember lightly those moments
heady with the heat and fragrance
of your skin.
And yet,
a black shawl of silk
your beauty clings endlessly
about my heart.

LOVE LETTERS

Turning cartwheels in the park
I catch you at all angles:
a tree sprouting from your shoulder
your back curved towards the grass
in laughter.

My best loved friend
though we cannot travel together
I will keep roadside shrines
tended for your shelter.
Round a bend, on some dusty highway
if you come upon a sudden green
and shining, there will be
the many polished icons
made in your absence
glowing for your welcome.

CODA

Poor woman, the man's truth
is an empty yabba for you.
Vainly you try to fill it
with a swirling, shifting
liquid of your own.

Where can we meet, my brother,
my lover, my friend
to make something new together.

> *I will meet you on the road*
> *for I have done with waiting.*
> *I will help you with your load*
> *and welcome your greeting.*
> *I will meet you on the road*
> *for I have shaped my journey.*

ELSA'S VERSION

Lawd God
I tired fe hear it
I tired fe hear it
so till.
All dem big talk:
"Women are our natural resources
Women are the backbone
of this country."
Me no bone inna
no body back
nor rib outa
no body side.
Is who dem tink
dey a go fool
while dem still a
treat we to no-count wages.
An we shouldn' mind
dat we riding fine
in nuff dutty song
a boom shaka boom
pon every street corner.

You rass man
stop put we down
in dutty song or
high-up editorial.
You can confuse, abuse
an mess wid you own self
till you good and ready
to deal wid I as
a real somebody.

Till day day come
        Lef me alone
        an me modda
        an me sista
        an me gal-pickney.

FOR ARTISTS AND WRITERS

So busy,
late night pushing at the windows.
Spouses, indignant or resigned,
register a mute petition
        or slam another door.
In the days,
jobs crowding out the sun
forced activity round the sullen clock.
When we meet
        warm enough smiles
        a calling card
We must meet sometime.
Sometime
        as the grey curls in your beard
        as his body thickens
and little webs trickle
from the corners of my eyes.
Sometime
        as the young man
        clothes his mind
with unshared songs.

We
writing black, the African experience,
        flinging accusations at our colonial past
        vying with each other to vault most quickly
the sharp european fence,
rushing to see
separately
whatever speaks of our warm, black roots.
Still the cold
creeps up through our careful behaviour.

It is at once more dangerous
and more safe
to pour ourselves onto our flat lovers
        who call us every night
        urging to be covered
to be owned by all the attention we reserve
lovingly for them.
Are we such lonely cowards?

It used to be enough
but I no longer want my portion
meted out.
I want now
        a frightened in the night child
        flinging wide the parent door
        an empty lover dry-eyed at the window
        a young mother howling in childbirth
        a farmer thundering down the drought.
Heavy, screaming want
to push past the cool that we are.

FOR ROBERTA FLACK & THE SISTERS

Black voice sing our new poetry.
Far off now, refined anguish oozing
from alexandrines, smothered in iambic
pentameters. Your words astride the music,
singing under skin "Love me baby."

Closed off by day, bossed by traffic
we forget, such release now, aural bridge
quickens, in a quiet room
grey mind, translucent nerves
journey to a half-remembered place.
A time when drum under leaves
flute over red savannah played
our cells into life.

There is a loneliness and sadness
between us black lovers. We are
of your poem, in your music yet,
we want to make together the poem
of your voice,
the breath of your pain.

Witness with us now, you
give the first reed, help us
to take hold, help us
to plait
the past
into our future.

MOUNTAIN LILIES AND SAND

I

A Victorian jug
handle akimbo on rounded hips
holds not larkspur or forsythia
but blue mountain lilies, small belled
colour tumbled from a hilly walk,
sprays from white-throated Victoria,
yellow day lilies, white arums,
one stalk of red, three open
and a bud.

At times
time seems so confused
I hardly know which century
I wriggle in. Worm on a line
between colours and cultures, yet
a china jug holds time and distance
in elegant symmetry.

Now, hearing the Polish violinist
I was again in a classroom
seeing red earth, green guangos,
in my head Verlaine singing

> *Les sanglots long*
> *Des violons*
> *De l'automne*

Kamau, the drum
new that should have been old
later shaped the clarity
of that child's absorption,
overlay it, gleaming turtle shell
on a soft, white oyster.

II

A coloured woman
married well,
a white man of charm, elegance
and erudition.
She worked, of course, while
he said goodbye
to the antiques, crystal, sold
to keep supporting his charm, elegance
and erudition.
She nursed, petted the child
but still at eighty-two
the soft oyster refuses to die
swallowing instead
every grain of her.

The black woman
who used to housekeep
till she too could not be paid
had six children. She kept
the local pretty boy, sleek
pants, new ganzie and long
little fingernail.
Bony little sprats, the children
gazed at his shelly gleam
and grew confused.

in an out de window
in an out
in an out de window
to see what you can see

Where now can we put
this clumsy anger? Laid
at the doorway of the past,
shaped as outside sins, it

flows over. Even
as we long for peace the ends trail
like veils between us.

I dropped a letter on de way
somebody pick it up
an neva give it back
not you, not you, but...

III

My friend tells me this dream
is not death but transition.
That mixture of eagerness and terror
wakes me now, a blue light
burning gaps in the search.
Not yet, for my brief past
spills out dazzling few times,
stepping over stretched bridge,
silence moving on the flow.

Standing on a dark hill
close behind rough chapel stones;
all beyond trees reached high
into the moist stars.

How the earth moved then,
just at that time!
There was, stirring, blowing
through the green black
something beyond pretty sounds
in a foreign language,
rolling on the drums
past the locks of Jah, flowing.

Crouched beside the potter
I see her dusty legs stretch,
her hands cradle up from her lap
a growing yabba. Made from earth,
buried in earth to fire.
We who were blessed
to sit with you that day,
glorious mother shaping
our tradition, we give thanks.

IV

Here a young future
building a present for us
from soil and wood.
Hear our song now, see
body stretched, mind
held in for that leap
across the drums,
dancer, across the drums
of Kumina and the rum bar.

Stretch wide your arms
for we are makers and made,
warm in spite of greed,
cruelty and despair,
the strokes – pen, shovel, brush
calling, see me now.
I who have been lost
am still seeking.

Your face, poem on a dancer's body
yours, blue eyes, dark skin,
yours, divine children,
yours, brother who rocks
my sick child
and yours black sister
and yours red sister
and mine.

We live
in mountain lilies and sand
dark hills, red plains.
In this short space
grouped together
in each other's time
we are flowing,
spilling past Garvey
giving praise
from the drum
singing
we are now

Scorched bamboo in the hills
whisper of old men
doubt, drought on evening path.
In a world with contact
brief as the silver dove
lighting her way home
here is reality
a dry whisper.

This man the poet carries his past
curled shells between his ribs
sun and growing coral under
his tongue and he is nourished.

The woman was a child
in a sweet dawn
cool and mist trailing
over shapeless trees.
Opening the window wide she put
her small child's tongue far into
the morning. It had a no-taste
breathlessness about it,
and she lulled dreamy at the sill.

Her present conjugates in
subjunctive, skimming down hills
dry as the first dusty moth of evening.

Bamboo in the hills
when a breeze rustles through
the sound is louder in its going.

I was born in this house
my children were born in this house
Eddie was born in this house.
If you see me coming
call my name.

Photos on the piano
layers of furniture
modern upholstered chair seats
and backs wedged on top of
old mahogany furniture,
the walls no-colour with age,
corners, surfaces piled with books,
papers, no subscription here to the
modern deity of disposable knowledge.

The rastas are oppressing me;
they walk into my house
through my land. Her voice
is soft, this outrage screams
in my head but her voice is soft.
If you see me coming
call my name.

A favourite daughter-in-law
came to stay at Christmas.
She knew, as the time approached,
she should move out of the spare
room where she had stayed to avoid
the stairs, but she was so tired.
When daughter-in-law came
it didn't matter (the first real
smile of the morning) she didn't
fuss her, just helped around.
Love and time in her eyes.

Two portraits of the artist
as a young man. One slender
dark and studious in cap and gown
somehow anonymous this first flight
with the status crow.
The other, direct, robust, looking
handsome – football hero eat-
your-heart-out girls.
If you see me coming
call my name.

A glass of cider, goodbyes
in the still room, presents
for the favourite daughter-in-law.
And I was standing at the bus stop
nobody's red chile on a strange street.
Across the street I saw the father
walking, held my breath as he
negotiated the traffic
and was magically beside me.

Why weep now for a brief moment,
a snatch of an old hand raised
in parting, such a small figure
on a busy street, a tailor's shop,
a child balanced in the square
of a window. Not parting, these images
not parting but greeting.
It does not matter now
that his name is not spoken
that his island does not sing
the praise songs he sings.

Here are the certainties, continuities
of time, place, he caught forever glowing.
The tailor's grandson will hear them

and know.
The red chile's granddaughter will hear them
and know.

Those of us bred in the pain and
homeless, hopelessness of other cities
will hear them and know.
If you see me coming
call my name,
soft, for I will hear.

UNSENT LETTERS

And of there is a space
in your going should I pile
more books on the shelf or lace
the quiet evenings with webs
of thought and could words trace
our fragments of time that curl
in soft scenarios wedded to place,
crisp but fragile in details of
you said I said and the ruffled race
against declaring too much.

And if there was tenderness deep
in the casual weave of more
coffee or would you like to sleep
now or should I go home but wait
another minute we could keep
these colours bright and the threads
of darker thoughts clipped, and sweep
under the bed those ragged ends
of moments trimmed to meet
your neatly ordered goals.

There is a space and I will miss
your kindness and if you write
I will answer and promise
not to be intense but keep
this pleasure in your friendship
gentle in my life.

STUDENT THOUGHTS AWAY FROM HOME

Far from you, all night
my life lies shaded
in a gloomy box. Tatters
of dreams, memories flutter
round my books, the bulb
harsh in my eyes, in my head.

Just before dawn, escaping
to the woods by the dam
I run, testing each foot, surprised
that my strength faces another day.
In this dull exile the day comes
soft as dragonflies, nervous skaters
past the soft plop, plopping
of leaping fish. Tiny clouds
winging from a cool sky settle
by water's edge, show legs, beaks,
egrets touched by the gold of sunrise.

Later, in the full rush of day
I walk soft, one moment of calm
shaped this fragile bowl I hold safe
till your coming should fill it.

NEW WORLD

Under stones, cracks,
the deeper level is moist;
trapped energy seeps into
roots. Thorn tree growing,
a tiny leap, a cell glowing:
thorn tree blooms in dust.

Over a cool, early morning lake
light slips up over the cleft
between mountains. Doves gleam
white in the gold, gone.
Gold, white, red sunrise
a miracle out of Genesis.

Mist in the trees
curls through hair, eyes
softness of September evening
deep in our blue hills.
We are a timeless people
in an ancient place
they call the New World.

TAKE AND HOLD

After weeks of mourning
(all the blues ever written
had lived in that time… I'm
so black and blue),
on a quiet morning
opening a window
peer heavy-lidded straight
into morning still dripping
with late night rain.
Banana birds busy in
a clump of smooth leaves.
Energy on the wing
colour at rest.

Padding through the empty house
open another window, clear crystals
hung on a line. A single alamanda
cups the early sun.
Behind, a row of houses fronting
the lane, quiet after last night's
slam domino game. Yesterday's shouts
to children, adults calling
"Eh… so how you doing…"
Quiet, wet and birds singing
in the morning.

Alone is a devious word
wail it golden on a sax
throb it deep on a drum
lilt it in counterpoint
on a silken piano. Together
all the loneness in one
finds harmony, balance in the others,

till alone become a song, a rhythm
that moves and beats and knocks
on a store of locked-up life.
Open the gate Legba
Atibon Legba, open the gate for us.

ABOUT THE AUTHOR

Christine Craig, was born in Kingston, Jamaica and spent much of her early years in rural St. Elizabeth, at the home of her grandparents, both of whom were teachers. She obtained a B.A. Honours in English and Mass Communications from the University of the West Indies, Mona, in 1980.

She is a short story writer and poet who also writes children's fiction. She has written several non fiction publications and training manuals on feminist and health issues. Her short stories and poems have been published in Caribbean, British and American anthologies and journals. In 1989 she was awarded a Fellowship to the International Writer's Program at the University of Iowa in Iowa City, Iowa.

Her first publications, *Emanuel and His Parrot*, and *Emanuel Goes to Market*, written for children, were a collaboration with her then husband, Jamaican artist Karl 'Jerry' Craig. She has written and directed a series of Jamaican history vignettes for children's television, and in 1990, Heinemann Caribbean published *Bird Gang*, a novella for children.

Her first collection of poetry, *Quadrille for Tigers*, was published in 1984. Her first collection of adult short stories, which deal with contemporary life, social mores and sexual politics in the Caribbean, *Mint Tea and Other Stories*, was published in 1993.

Craig has been a lifelong campaigner for human rights and environmental protection. She was instrumental in setting up the Women's Bureau in the 1980's, for governmental and non-governmental protection of women's rights in Jamaica. Along with Denis Watson, she co-authored *Guyana at the Crossroads*, 1992 and she co-edited Jamaica's National Report to the Word Conference on the Environment, Rio de Janeiro.

She tutored English Literature at the University of the West Indies in the 1990s and was Adjunct Professor of Fiction and Commercial Writing at Barry University, Miami, Florida. From 1990 to 1998, she was Miami Editor of *The Jamaica Gleaner* in Miami, Florida, responsible for news and features.

She lives in Fort Lauderdale, Florida.